PRACTICAL GUIDE TO
NORTHERN IDAHO'S WILD EDIBLE PLANTS

STEVEN C. GOLIEB

edible wilds
EDIBLE WILDS LLC

PUBLISHED BY
EDIBLE WILDS BOOKS
A SUBSIDIARY OF
LEO LASAGNA LLC
BAKER CITY, OR

Library of Congress Cataloging-in-Publication Data

Golieb, Steven C. (Date__)
    A Practical Guide to Idaho's Wild Edible Plants. --1st Edition
        p. cm.
    ISBN 0692734996

Back cover photography by: Lindsey Stallings Elem, www.lindseyelem.com

Photos including Amaranth, Cattail, Clover, Burdock (small), Dandelion, Sunflower, Thistle, Salsify (small), Rose, Purslane, Plantain, Willow, Oak, Maple, Juniper, Cottonwood, Blue Spruce and Aspen were taken by Steven C. Golieb. All other photos in book, unless otherwise noted, are sourced by Wikipedia.Org

This book was made in conjunction with Edible Wilds, LLC of Eden, UT

www.ediblewilds.us

www.leolasagna.com

For my perfect and beautiful son Jacob.

CONTENTS

INTRODUCTION

Hello, and thank you for picking up this book! My name is Steven Golieb, and I am a specialist in edible and medicinal wild plants. I am the owner of Edible Wilds, LLC of Eden, UT, a company that produces food products from edible wild plants harvested locally in the Rocky Mountains. I give guided tours and seminars on how to survive in the wild eating exclusively from the native vegetation.

The need for this book became apparent after endless and unfruitful searches for information on wild vegetation specific to individual states. All other books and guides available are aimed towards broad regions, such as the Rocky Mountain region, which spans over 3,000 miles over two countries and has a range of elevation of 14,440 feet high to as low as sea level. Clearly there are an overwhelming range of species and ecosystems that can inhabit that vast and diverse expansion of land. When focusing locally, however, the guides become almost entirely irrelevant; they become difficult to apply to specific areas (such as states) and contain a surplus of information that's hard to sift through. I felt the need to create a *practical* guide—one that could actually be of use to the Idaho wilderness and urban areas exclusively.

This book includes pictures, descriptions, and practical information on how to prepare and consume the different species available to the area. With each species represented in this book, a useful key is provided (left).

As you can see from the key sample (left), each species is star-rated on its abundance (how easy it is to find and how common a species it is to the area). The key also provides the seasons the species is available for harvest, its scientific information, as well as nutritional info. This feature makes finding a wild meal efficient, easy, and exciting!

Abundance: ⭐⭐⭐⭐
Seasons: **Spring**
Common Name: **Thistle**
Scientific Name: **Cirsium**
Family: **Asteraceae**
Nutrition:

-Fiber
-Ascorbic Acid*
-Chlorogenic Acid*
-Potassium*
-Inulin*
-Protein
-Calcium
-Cinarina*

* = Very high amounts

Many of the plants local to Idaho have great medicinal purposes and properties. The medicinal uses are represented in the "Wild Medicine" section of the book.

There are many great benefits to learning about native plants and trees. Whether for survival, for fun, or for natural healing purposes, a great feeling of comfort and confidence can come from knowing ones surroundings while in nature. I sincerely hope this book can assist in better understanding nature, and hopefully that understanding can lead to a passion and furthered curiosity. Enjoy, and safe eating!

A WARNING

Before voyaging out in your neighborhood or in the wild in search for food, please take into consideration a few safety tips to ensure a successful and healthy harvest.

1) WEED KILLERS AND PESTICIDES-- Make sure to check for signs of spraying. If you are in an urban area, it is common for lawns and fields to be sprayed by chemicals. Make sure you are careful in what you harvest. Common signs of spraying is patches of dead weeds, browning of the leaves, and an abnormal change in height and health of the plant. It's also always a good policy to wash all harvested goods in water.
2) POISONOUS VARIETIES-- Most of the plants in this book have no "look-a-likes", or plants that are poisonous that resemble the edible ones. However, always take precautions. If you aren't sure what you're eating and you feel there's a chance it could be a different plant than the one in the book, just leave it alone. It's not worth risking it.
3) GENERAL RULE OF THUMB-- Though there are exceptions, and unless characterized in the description of the plant/tree in this book, the following are typical characteristics of poisonous plants and should be avoided:
   1. Milky or discolored sap
   2. Spines, fine hairs, or thorns
   3. Beans, bulbs, or seeds inside pods
   4. Bitter or soapy taste
   5. Dill or parsnip looking leaves
   6. "Almond" scent in the woody parts and leaves
   7. Grain heads with pink, purplish, or black spurs
   8. Three-leaved growth pattern
4) BUGS-- Many of the species mentioned in this book are frequented by a variety of insects. Make sure to wash all harvested goods thoroughly, and double check to make sure you've removed all insects. Many bugs can be poisonous or can cause severe sickness.

All in all, harvesting and consuming edible wilds plants is a very safe and fun activity. Just make sure you're taking precautions and you'll be just fine. Enjoy!

EDIBLE PLANTS

Amaranth

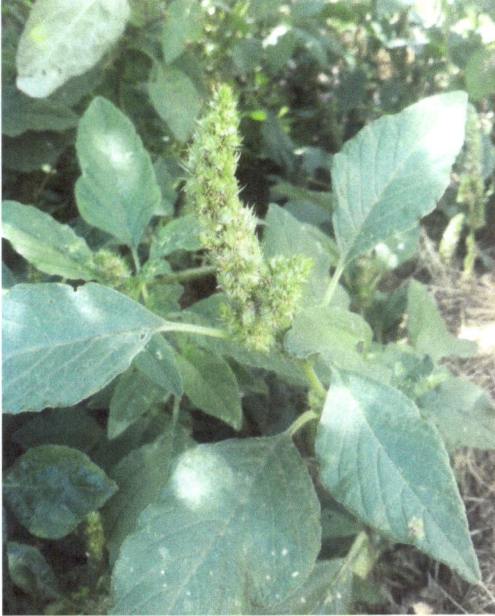

Abundance: ⭐⭐⭐
Seasons: **Spring, Summer**
Common Name: **Amaranth**
Scientific Name: **Amaranthus**
Family: **Amaranthaceae**
Nutrition:

-Vitamin E*
-Flavanoids*
-Calcium*
-Mangesium*
-Fatty acids*
-Vitamin A*
-Vitamin C*
-Manganese
-Magnesium

* = Very high amounts

Native to the Americas, all parts of the Amaranth plant are edible. The leaves of the plant contain oxalic acid. Although the acid is not poisonous and you may eat the plant raw, it is recommended to boil leaves in water to remove the acid. Do not use left over water. Amaranth can be found in well shaded or watered areas. They are very common weeds in gardens and lawns.

Roots: **N/A**
Leaves: **Edible**
Seeds: **Edible**
Stalks: **Edible**
Flowers/Buds: **Edible**

Practical Applications:
1) All parts of the plant can be eaten raw, though the leaves should be eaten in moderation due to presence of oxalic acid. If boiled, all parts of the plant can be eaten regularly.

Balsamroot

Abundance: ★★
Seasons: **Spring, Summer**
Common Name: **Arrow-leaved Balsamroot**
Scientific Name: **Balsamorhiza Sagittata**
Family: **Asteraceae**
Nutrition:

-Riboflavin*
-Omega Fatty Acids
-Phosphorus*
-Copper*
-Manganese*
-Magnesium*
-Potassium
-Protein*

-Fiber
-Iron*
-Pantothenic Acid
-Vitamin B6*
-Niacin*
-Thiamin*

* = Very high amounts

Balsamroot is a relative of the Sunflower plant native to the western Americas. All parts of the plant are edible. The plant was "discovered" in 1806 by an explorer near the Lewis and Clark Pass WARNING: Do not confuse with poisonous Arnica plant, which can cause severe internal issues. Arrow-leaved Balsamroot can be found on dry mountain slopes.

Roots: **Edible**
Leaves: **Edible**
Seeds: **Edible**
Stalks: **Edible**
Flowers/Buds: **Edible**

Practical Applications:
1. The young stems and leaf stocks can be eaten raw or cooked, along with peeled roots. It is recommended to always cook the plant. Roots are more sweet when cooked with a low temperature for a long period of time.
2. Seeds can be dried and ground into meal, or they can be roasted.
3. Roots can be stored for long periods of time. First cook, then dry, then store in a dry place. They can be reconstituted by soaking them overnight or boiled.

Bedstraw

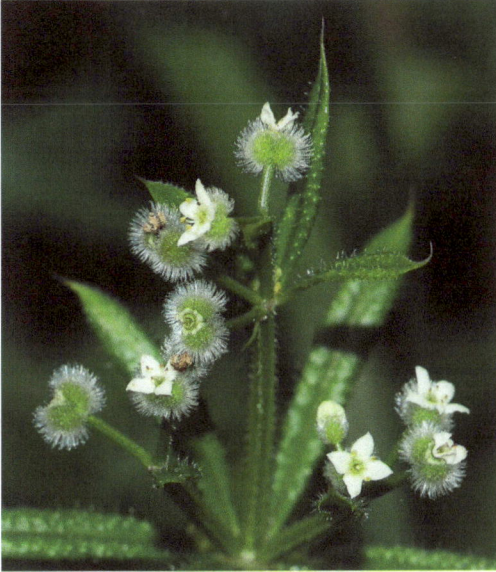

Abundance: ★★★★
Seasons: **Spring, Summer**
Common Names: **Cleaver, goosegrass, stickyweed**
Scientific Name: **Galium aparine**
Family: **Rubiaceae**
Nutrition:

-Vitamin C*

Additional nutritional information not known

* = Very high amounts

The majority of this extremely common plant is edible. Being a somewhat of a pest to people who come in contact with it, it is easily recognizable as it will stick to clothes and even to itself. With many hairs on the plant, it can be found in fields all throughout the state—typically in areas with more moisture. Eating the plant in large quantities can cause mild stomach issues as it can be used as a laxative.

Roots: **Not Edible**
Leaves: **Edible**
Stalks: **Edible**
Flowers/Buds/Seeds: **Edible**

Practical Applications:
1. The leaves, stems and flowers of the plant are edible, although it is best to harvest the plant before it fruits. Younger plants are best to eat raw as older plants become very unpalatable due to texture. Plant can be cooked through boiling or mixing with meats or other vegetables. Great source of Vitamin C.

Bergamot (Wild)

Abundance: ⭐⭐⭐
Seasons: **Spring Summer Fall**
Common Names: **Bee Balm**
Scientific Name: **Monarda fistulosa**
Family: **Lamiaceae**
 Nutrition:

-Vitamin A
-Iron
-Manganese

Additional nutritional information not known

* = Very high amounts

Wild Bergamot is an extremely common and widely used medicinal plant in the mint family. Native Americans used this plant to treat cold and flu symptoms, as poultices for treating skin infections and minor wounds, to treat mouth and throat infections, to treat for worms and parasites, and to protect meat from bugs. Wild Burgamot can be found all over the state, but primarily in the areas with more rainfall. Can be found in fields, foothills, and vacant properties. Plant smells strongly of mint.

Roots: **N/A**
Leaves: **Edible (see below)**
Stalks: **Edible (see below)**
Flowers/Buds/Seeds: **Edible (see below)**

Practical Applications:
1. This plant is typically used medicinally, but it can also be made into a strong tea (usually sweetened with honey). Tea can be made from all parts of the plant, but usually from dried and stored flowers.
2. Dried leaves can be crushed and applied to meat to repel insects.

Black Raspberry

Abundance: ⭐⭐⭐
Seasons: **Summer**
Common Name: **Blackberry**
Scientific Name: **Rubus Occidentalis**
Family: **Rosaceae**
Nutrition:

-Vitamin E*
-Folate*
-Magnesium*
-Copper*
-Dietary Fibers*
-Potassium*
-Vitamin C*
-Vitamin K*
-Maganese*

* = Very high amounts

Black raspberry are a cross between blackberries and raspberries and are native to North America. Very common throughout New England, black raspberries can be found on the edges of fields or pastures and in sunny areas. Black raspberries provide a great source of antioxidants and nutrition.

Leaves: **Medicinal**
Fruit: **Edible**
Stalk: **Edible - Young (see below)**

Practical Applications:
1) Berries can be eaten raw and are ripe throughout summer. They can be made into jams.
2) Leaves can be made into a tea but are mostly medicinal.
3) Very young shoots can be eaten and used in salads.

Bugleweed

Abundance: ⭐⭐⭐
Seasons: **Spring Summer**
Common Names: **waterhorehound, gypsywort**
Scientific Name: **Lycopus**
Family: **Lamiaceae**
Nutrition:

-Vitamin A
-Iron
-Manganese

Additional nutritional information not known

* = Very high amounts

Bugleweed is a member of the mint family and can be found in areas of moisture, including lakes, streams, and marshes. This plant is mostly harvested for its roots, which can be eaten raw, although are best steamed or boiled. It is best to gather the roots in springtime.

Roots: **Edible**
Leaves: **Not Edible**
Stalks: **Not Edible**
Flowers/Buds/Seeds: **Not Edible**

Practical Applications:
1. The roots of the bugleweed plant are edible raw and are best to be harvested in the spring. As they get older they are good to boil or steam. The roots can also be dried for storage.

Burdock

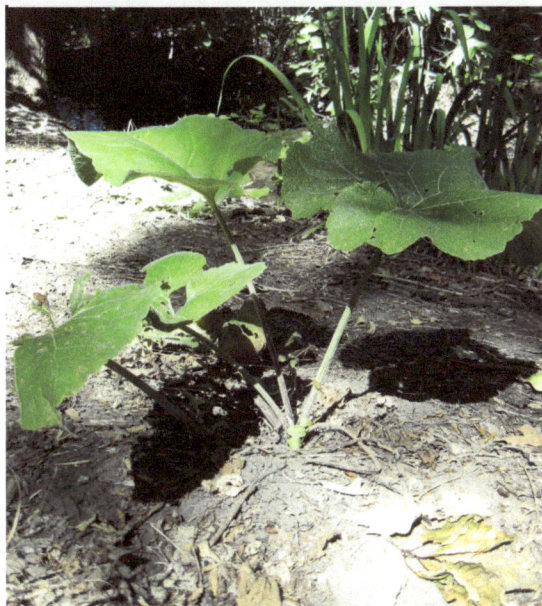

Abundance: ⭐⭐⭐
Seasons: **Spring, Summer**
Common Name: **Burdock**
Scientific Name: **Arctium**
Family: **Asteraceae**
Nutrition:

```
-Fiber*
-Phytosterols*
-Essential Fatty Acids*
-Calcium*
-Amino Acids*
-Potassium*
-Iron
-Protein
-Maganese

* = Very high amounts
```

Burdock is a relative of artichoke and has been used as a medicinal plant for thousands of years. It has been used as a blood purifier and kidney and liver cleanser, and its oils have been used for scalp treatment. Burdock can be found in many fairly-watered fields, abandoned lawns, forests and riverbanks. In summer Burdock produces a pink-colored flower that turns into a brown bur. This plant is considered invasive by many because of its burs.

Roots: **Edible**
Leaves: **Edible, not recommended**
Seeds: **Edible, not recommended**
Stalk: **Edible**

Practical Applications:
1) Burdock root is the most practical part of plant to eat. Dig out roots deep (do not try to pull out of ground, as it will break the stalk). Wash off roots and boil in water. Great source of essential vitamins and minerals, and it actually tastes great! Resembles flavor of artichoke and cauliflower.
2) Flower stalks can be harvested in spring before they mature or flower. Peel stalks thoroughly and eat raw.

Cattail

Abundance: ★★★★
Seasons: Spring, **Summer**
Common Name: **Corn Dog Grass**
Scientific Name: **Typha**
Family: **Typhaceae**
Nutrition:

-Iron
-Phosphorus
-Dietary Fiber*
-Vitamin K*
-Vitamin B6*
-Calcium*
-Magnesium*
-Potassium
-Maganese

* = Very high amounts
** The nutritional info is for leaf
shoots only.

Cattail is a very common and multifaceted survival food. Every part of the plant is edible and it provides a filling and nutritious meal. Cattails can be found near lakes, streams, river, ponds, bays and stagnant water all throughout Idaho.

Roots: **Edible**
Leaves: **Edible**
Flowers/Seeds/Pollen: **Edible**
Stalk: **Edible**

Practical Applications:
1) The inner white core of cattail roots can be eaten raw or cooked. It can also be made into syrup or fermented to make alcohol.
2) Young shoots can be eaten raw, but do not mistaken with the iris plant, which is poisonous.
3) When plant is in active pollination, pollen may be collected and used as flour. Green flower sprouts can be boiled and eaten as corn-on-the-cob. Seeds can be ground as a flour or used in soups or breads

Catnip

Abundance: ★★★★
Seasons: Spring, **Summer**
Common Name: **Catswort catmint**
Scientific Name: **Nepeta cataria**
Family: **Lamiaceae**
Nutrition:

Nutritional facts unknown

Catnip is extremely common throughout the state. Originally native to Europe, the Middle East and central Asia, the plant has spread in both the wild and has been cultivated as an ornamental plant in gardens. It's known for being drought and deer resistant and for its medicinal and practical uses, such as insect repellent.

Roots: **Not Edible**
Leaves: **Edible (see below)**
Flowers: **Edible (see below)**
Stalk: Not **Edible (only dried as seasoning)**

Practical Applications:
1. Young leaves are edible raw when young, while older leaves can be dried and used as seasoning.
2. Dried flowers can be made into a tea, which has medicinal properties.
3. Oil from the leaves have been used as an insect repellent against flies and mosquito's.

Chickweed

Abundance: ★★★★
Seasons: **Summer, Fall, Winter**
Common Name: **Common chickweeed**
Scientific Name: **Stellaria media**
Family: **Caryophyllaceae**

Nutrition:

-Vitamin A*
-Vitamin C*

* = Very high amounts
** The nutritional info is for leavy vegetation only.

Chickweed is a very common ground cover that can be found throughout the entire state primarily in lawns, disturbed areas and in valleys (lower elevation). The stem has a single line of hairs running between each stem node. Mostly available in late summer, fall and early winter, chickweed is an excellently flavored food high in nutrients similar to that of spinach. Although a rare occurrence, limit the amount of consumption due to the presence of saponins, which can be toxic. It is edible both raw and cooked like spinach.

Roots: **N/A**
Leaves: **Edible**
Flowers: **Edible**
Stalk: **Edible**

Practical Applications:
1. The whole plant can be collected and eaten raw or boiled. Cooked leaves are considered safer to eat by some, as well as the quality of taste improving.

Chicory

Abundance: ⭐⭐⭐
Seasons: **Spring, Summer**
Common Name: **Blue Daisy**
Scientific Name: **Cichorium intybus**
Family: **Asteraceae**

Nutrition:

-Niacin*
-Chromium*
-Calcium*
-Mangesium*
-Phosphorus*
-Vitamin C*
-Potassium*
-Thiamine
-Magnesium*

* = Very high amounts

Chicory is a commonly-found plant throughout the northwest. They can be found in undisturbed fields or sides of the road. The whole plant is edible—the flowers, leaves and the roots. The leaves resemble that of dandelions. Flowers appear in late spring and during the summer.

Roots: **Edible**
Leaves: **Edible**
Flowers: E**dible**
Seeds: **Edible**

Practical Applications:
1) The relatively large taproots are edible—they can be roasted or cooked as a vegetable. Roots are often used as a coffee substitute when roasted.
2) Leaves should be eaten in spring as they are easily digestible and more palatable. Can be eaten raw. Can also be boiled as a vegetable.
3) Flowers can be eaten raw or boiled.

Clover

Abundance:⭐⭐⭐
Seasons: **Spring, Summer**
Common Name: **Clover**
Scientific Name: **Trifolium**
Family: **Fabaceae**
Nutrition:

-Niacin*
-Chromium*
-Calcium*
-Mangesium*
-Phosphorus*
-Vitamin C*
-Potassium*
-Thiamine
-Magnesium*

* = Very high amounts

Clover is an incredible survival food often found in urban and wild areas throughout Idaho—mostly found in lawns or more watered areas. Originally introduced from Europe, three varieties of clover now grow throughout the United States, including Idaho. The above picture is white clover, the most commonly-found clover in Idaho.

Roots: **Edible, not recommended**
Leaves: **Edible, best in spring**
Flowers: E**dible**
Seeds: **Edible**

Practical Applications:
1. Flowers can be eaten raw, fried or sauteed. They can also be used to make teas and wines or dried and ground into a flour. They can also be added to soups.
2. Leaves should be eaten in moderation unless cooked, as they are often difficult to digest. Leaves are best in springtime.
3. Roots are not recommended to eat, though they can be eaten after cooked.
4. Seeds can be ground into a flour or used medicinally.

Cocklebur

Abundance: ⭐⭐⭐
Seasons: **Spring, Summer**
Common Name: **Cocklebur**
Scientific Name: **Xanthium strumarium**
Family: **Asteraceae**
Nutrition:

Not enough info is known.

* = Very high amounts

Cocklebur is a common plant found throughout the state. It is capable of living in dry and moist climates. It has been used medicinally and as a food source by native populations throughout the world. Although common, this plant cannot be consumed in large quantities as there are potentially poisonous chemicals in the plant. There have been reported deaths and illnesses when consumed in large quantities.

Roots: **Not Edible**
Leaves: **Edible, see below**
Flowers: **Not Edible**
Seeds: **Edible**

Practical Applications:
1. Young leaves are edible when cooked—thoroughly boiled. Change water a couple of times when boiling to ensure potentially toxic chemicals are removed. Uncooked leaves are poisonous.
2. Seeds of the plant are edible raw, but be sure to limit consumption. They can be ground into a flour as well.

Cranberry

Abundance: ⭐
Seasons: **Fall, Winter**
Common Name: **Curly Dock**
Scientific Name: **Rumex crispus**
Family: **Buckwheat/Smartweed**

Nutrition:

-Vitamin E*
-Magnesium*
-Copper*
-Dietary Fibers*
-Potassium*
-Vitamin C*
-Vitamin K*
-Maganese*

* = Very high amounts

Cranberries are a wonderful treat to stumble upon, though they are not very common in more developed areas. Shown to have antibacterial properties, cranberries are both nutritious as well as medicinal. They can be found growing in very well watered areas and can be harvested throughout fall and winter.

Roots: **Not Edible**
Leaves: **Not Edible**
Fruit: **Edible Cooked**
Stalk: **Not Edible**

Practical Applications:
1) Cranberries are extremely bitter and sour and should be eaten cooked. Can be made into jams, juices or whole.

Dandelion

Abundance: ⭐⭐⭐⭐⭐
Seasons: **Spring, Summer**
Common Name: **Common Dandelion**
Scientific Name: **Taraxacum O.**
Family: **Asteraceae**
Nutrition:

-Fiber*
-Vitamin A*
-Vitamin C*
-Calcium
-Phosphorus*
-Potassium
-Iron*
-Protein*
-Beta Carotene*
-Maganese

-Vitamin E*
-Vitamin K*
-Thiamin
-Riboflavin*
-Vitamin B6*

* = Very high amounts

Dandelion is by far one of the most nutritious and common plants found in Idaho. Every plant of the dandelion is edible and is extremely beneficial. Be sure that you are harvesting dandelion safe from weed killers and/or other lawn chemicals.

Roots: **Edible**
Leaves: **Edible, best in spring**
Seeds: **Edible, not recommended**
Flowers: **Edible**
Stalk: E**dible**

Practical Applications:
   1) Leaves can be eaten raw and used as a salad. They are less bitter and most tender during springtime.
   2) Roots can be eaten raw, boiled, fried or dried and grounded. Roots can also create a wonderful medicinal tea.
   3) Flowers are edible and can be eaten raw. They can also make a great tea or can be used for coloring.

False Solomon's Seal

Abundance: ⭐⭐⭐⭐
Seasons: **Spring, Summer, Fall**
Common Name: **Treacleberry**
Scientific Name: **Maianthemum Racemosum**
Family: **Asparagaceae**
Nutrition:

Currently Unknown

False solomon's seal is a very common plant found throughout the state and provides a good source of food throughout the warmer months. The plant is extremely medicinal and very easy to digest. It can be found in forests, riverbanks, clearings and more.

Leaves: **Edible, best in spring**
Fruit: **Edible**
Roots: **Edible — Not Recommended**

Practical Applications:
1) Very young leaves can be eaten raw or cooked. Can be added to salads.
2) Berries are ripe and turn red in summer. Berries can be eaten raw.
3) Roots are edible but are not recommended—they must be soaked in lye and parboiled.

Fiddlehead Ferns

Abundance: ⭐⭐⭐
Seasons: **Spring**
Common Name: **Bracken**
Scientific Name: **Pteridium aquilinum**
Family: **Dennstaedtiaceae**
Nutrition:

-Vitamin A*
-Vitamin C*
-Potassium
-Iron
-Manganese
-Copper
-Omega-3*
-Omega-6

* = Very high amounts

Fiddlehead ferns, also known as bracken and ostrich fern, are quite abundant in the Pacific Northwest. There are many varieties that can be found anywhere from foothills to wet areas, such as next to rivers, ponds, etc. They typically like to grow in areas with a lot of moisture. These ferns are ONLY edible in spring when they are coiled (as seen above) and when outer skins are removed. Eating these ferns in consistently large quantities or when the plant is mature can be dangerous to your health.

Leaves/stalk: **Edible, spring only**

Practical Applications:
1) Take whole fern coil (as seen above), remove outer casing, and soak in water to remove bitterness. Best when boiled in a couple changes of water. Eat whole.
2) Fiddleheads can also be stored by drying. They can be reconstituted with water, roasted or ground into a flour.

Fireweed

Abundance: ⭐⭐
Seasons: **Spring Summer Fall**
Common Name: **Fireweed**
Scientific Name: **Chamerion angustifolium**
Family: **Onagraceae**

Nutrition:

-Manganese*
-Calcium
-Folate
-Magnesium
-Vitamin B6
-Vitamin A
-Niacin
-Dietary Fiber

* = Very high amounts
** The nutritional info is for leavy vegetation only.

There really isn't much better than stumbling upon a nice field of fireweed plants when foraging in the wilderness; besides being a beautiful plant, almost every part of the plant is edible raw and actually tastes alright! There are a couple of varieties that grow throughout the Pacific Northwest. Be sure to notice the unique vein structure of fireweed before consuming in spring, as it can be confused with toxic look-a-likes in the lily family. The plant, when consumed in large quantities, can act as a laxative.

Leaves: **Edible**
Flowers: **Edible**
Stalks/Shoots: **Edible**

Practical Applications:
1) The young leaves and shoots of the plant can be eaten raw.
2) Flowers can be edible raw, and flower bud clusters can be consumed when cooked as a vegetable.
3) Stem piths can be added to soups as a thickener.

Grape – Wild

Abundance: ⭐⭐
Seasons: **Spring, Summer, Fall**
Common Name: **River Bank Grape**
Scientific Name: **Vitis Riparia**
Family: **Vitis**

Nutrition:

-Dietary Fiber*
-Manganese*
-Selenium*
-Iron*
-Niacin
-Thiamin
-Folate
-Phosphorus

* = Very high amounts

Wild grapes grown on thorn-less vines can be found on trees or structures. The leaves are generally heart shaped, are coarsely toothed and lobed. Both the fruits and the leaves grow directly off of the stems. Fruits have multiple seeds inside of the dark purple berries. There are multiple varieties of wild grape, so appearances may vary slightly.

Leaves: **Edible, best in spring and early summer**
Fruit: **Edible**
Roots: **Not Edible**

Practical Applications:
1. The berries can be eaten raw or cooked, including using the berries to make jam. The berries can be harvested in fall.
2. Young leaves can be collected, boiled and used as a wrap to eat other foods such as meat or rice.

Great Mullein

Abundance: ★★★★
Seasons: **Spring, Summer**
Common Name: **Common Mullein**
Scientific Name: **Verbascum Thapsus**
Family: **Scrophulariaceae**
Nutrition:

Currently Unknown

* = Very high amounts

A very common plant of the United States, the great mullein is mostly medicinal but the leaves can be made into a tea. The tea must be taken in moderation and is recommended to only be used medicinally. The seeds are toxic and should never be ingested.

Roots: **Not Edible**
Leaves: **Edible - Medicinal**
Seeds: **Poisonous**
Flowers: **Not Edible**
Stalk: **Not Edible**

Practical Applications:
1) Leaves can be boiled into a tea. However, tea MUST be strained multiple times to protect throat against tiny fibers on leaves as they can cause irritation.

Huckleberry

Abundance:⭐⭐⭐
Seasons: **Summer**
Common Name: **Huckleberry**
Scientific Name: **Vaccinium**
Family: **Ericaceae**
Nutrition:

High in Polyphenols and Anthocyanin

* = Very high amounts

A very common plant of the state of Idaho, Huckleberry is a delicacies and nutrition packed

Roots: **Not Edible**
Leaves: **Edible - Medicinal**
Seeds: **Poisonous**
Flowers: **Not Edible**
Stalk: **Not Edible**

Practical Applications:
  1. Leaves can be boiled into a tea. However, tea MUST be strained multiple times to protect throat against tiny fibers on leaves as they can cause irritation.

Jerusalem Artichoke

Abundance: ⭐⭐⭐
Seasons: **Fall, Winter, Spring**
Common Name: **Sun Root**
Scientific Name: **Helianthus tuberosus**
Family: **Asteraceae**

Nutrition:

-Thiamin*
-Phosphorous*
-Potassium*
-Iron*
-Inulin*
-Vitamin C
-Niacin
-Pantothenic Acid
-Vitamin B6
-Copper
-Dietary Fiber

* = Very high amounts

A very common plant of the north eastern United States, the Jerusalem artichoke is an incredible survival plant. As a survival mechanism, the plant stores all of its energy into tubers, or roots, much like sweet potato or yams. Jerusalem artichokes resemble the sunflower plant and can be found in disturbed areas such as roadsides or fields.

Roots (tubers): **Edible**
Leaves: **Not Edible**
Flowers: **Not Edible**
Stalk: **Not Edible**

Practical Applications:
1) The tubers can be harvested by digging them out from fall to early spring. They can be used exactly like a potato—boiled, roasted, baked, steamed, sauteed, etc. They can also be thinly cut and mixed with salads.

Knotweed

Abundance: ⭐⭐⭐⭐⭐
Seasons: **Summer, Fall**
Common Name: **Common knotgrass, pigweed, birdweed**
Scientific Name: **Polygonum**
Family: **Polygonaceae**
Nutrition:

Nutritional information not available

* = Very high amounts

A very common plant throughout the majority of the United States, knotweed is a low-growing weed that typically grows in cracks of sidewalks, gardens, lawns, and more. It usually becomes tougher in texture as the season progresses. Raw plants eaten in large amounts can cause diarrhea or upset stomach. Best to cook (see below).

Roots: **N/A**
Leaves/stalks: **Edible**
Flowers: **Edible**
Seeds: E**dible**

Practical Applications:
1. The whole plant (above ground) can be eaten raw in very small quantities, but should otherwise be cooked (boiled, in soups, etc).
2. The seeds of the plant can be eaten whole or grounded into a meal.

Lamb's Quarters

Abundance: ⭐⭐⭐
Seasons: **Spring, Summer**
Common Name: **Pigweed**
Scientific Name: **Chenopodium Album**
Family: **Chenopodiaceae**

Nutrition:

-Niacin*   -Riboflavin*
-Folate*   -Vitamin B6*
-Iron*   -Calcium*
-Magnesium*   -Potassium*
-Phosphorus*   -Copper*
-Dietary Fiber*   -Manganese*
-Protein*
-Vitamin A*

* = Very high amounts

Extremely similar in taste and texture to spinach and closely related to Quinoa, lamb's quarters are extremely rich in nutrients and are a valuable survival plant. However, similar to curly dock and spinach, lamb's quarters is high in oxalic acid and should be eaten in moderation or boiled to remove the acid. Lamb's quarters can be found in more watered areas such as garden areas.

Roots: **N/A**
Leaves: **Edible, best in spring**
Seeds: **Edible**
Flowers: **Edible**
Stalk: **Edible**

Practical Applications:
1) Lamb's quarters leaves and stalks can be eaten raw or boiled and have similar taste to spinach.
2) Seeds can be eaten raw, grounded and can be used for sprouting. Lambs quarters seeds have been found in ancient archeological sites.
3) Flower clusters can be eaten raw or can be added to soups.

Miner's Lettuce

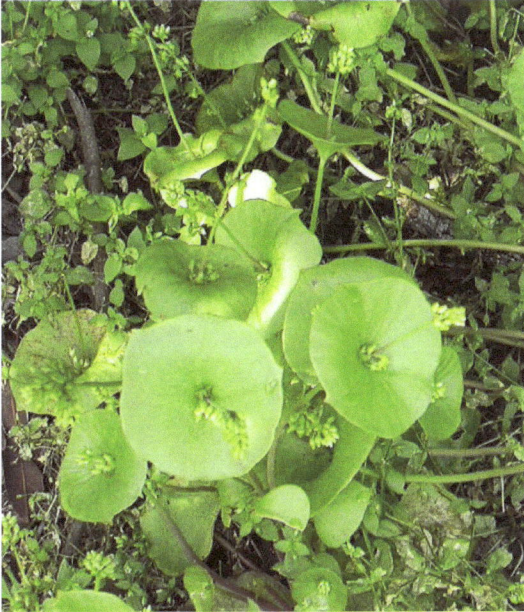

Abundance: ⭐⭐⭐
Seasons: **Spring, Summer**
Common Name: **Indian's lettuce, winter purslane, miner's lettuce**
Scientific Name: **Claytonia perfoliata**
Family: **Montiaceae**
Nutrition:

-Vitamin C*
-Beta Carotene
-Protein

* = Very high amounts

Miner's lettuce got its name due to the popular consumption from miner's during the Calidornia Gold Rush. It was used to prevent scurvy due to the plant's high amount of vitamin C. Mostly fond in moist wooded areas and fields. All parts of the plant are edible raw or cooked.

Roots: **Edible (not recommended)**
Leaves: **Edible**
Seeds: **Edible**
Flowers: **Edible**
Stalk: E**dible**

Practical Applications:
1. All parts of the plant are edible either raw or cooked. When boiled, taste and texture resembles that of spinach.

Mint – wild

Abundance: ★★★★
Seasons: **Spring, Summer**
Common Name: **Mint**
Scientific Name: **Mentha**
Family: **Lamiaceae**
Nutrition:

-Vitamin A
-Iron
-Manganese

* = Very high amounts

Mint is a commonly-found plant throughout the entire state. There are many varieties that can be found, including spearmint and peppermint. They are typically found in areas of the state with higher rainfall in fields, foothills and mountainous regions.

Leaves: **Edible - Young**
Flowers: **Edible**
Stalk: **Edible**

Practical Applications:
1) The mint plant is primarily used as a seasoning, but can be eaten raw.
2) Dried and crushed/powdered leaves can be spread over berries and/or meat to repel insects.

Mustard

Abundance: ⭐⭐⭐
Seasons: **Spring, Summer**
Common Name: **Wintercress, True Mustard, Tumble-mustard, Tansy-mustard**
Scientific Name: **Brassica**
Family: **Brassicaceae**
Nutrition:

Unknown for wild varieties

* = Very high amounts

There are over 3200 species in the mustard family (Brassicaceae) worldwide, including broccoli, cabbage, radish, turnip and cauliflower. However, identifying members of the mustard family is relatively simple: the flowers must consist of 4 pedals, 4 sepals, 4 tall stamens, 2 short stamens and one pistil. The most common color for wild mustard flowers is yellow. The plant can be found all over the state, but is more common in areas of more moisture and rain. Search for the plant in fields, plains, disturbed areas, etc.

Seeds: Edible
Leaves: **Edible**
Flowers: **Edible**
Stalk: E**dible**

Practical Applications:
1. The whole plant can be cooked as cooked greens. The more mature the plant is the more bitter it becomes. Boil in in two changes of water to reduce bitterness.

Oregon Grapes

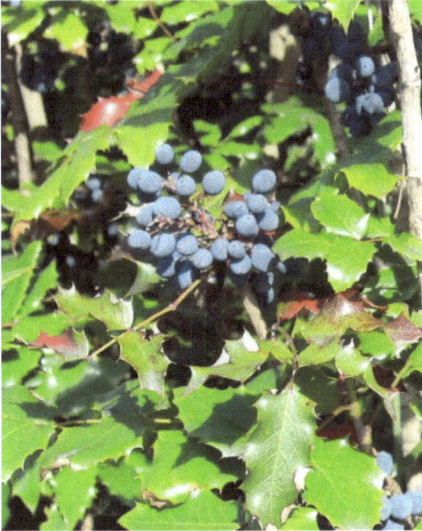

Abundance: ⭐⭐
Seasons: **Spring, Summer**
Common Name: **Pigweed**
Scientific Name: **Mahonia Aquifolium**
Family: **Berberidaceae**
Nutrition:

-Pectin*
-Vitamin A*
-Vitamin C*

* = Very high amounts

Idaho grapes are often a common ornamental plant that can be found in urban areas and in the wild. Though both edible and extremely medicinal, Idaho grapes should be avoided by pregnant women and should not be ingested when experiencing diarrhea. Berries should be eaten in moderation.

Roots: **Edible - Medicinal**
Leaves: **Edible - Young**
Flowers: **Edible**
Fruits: **Edible**
Stalk: **Not Edible**

Practical Applications:
1. Berries can be eaten raw, though they can be quite sour. They can be used to make jams, wine, or juices. The berries are full of antioxidants.
2. Very young and tender leaves can be eaten raw or boiled.
3. The roots are primarily medicinal and should only be really used as such, but they are edible if boiled.
4. The flowers are quite sour but can be added to foods for flavoring, such as salads or soups.

Pansy (Violet)

Abundance: ⭐⭐⭐
Seasons: **Spring, Summer**
Common Name: **Wintercress,
True Mustard, Tumble-
mustard, Tansy-mustard**
Scientific Name: **Brassica**
Family: **Brassicaceae**
Nutrition:

Unknown nutritional information.

* = Very high amounts

There are multiple varieties of violet that grow in the
Pacific Northwest, including the most commonly known Pansy,
along with Canada Violet, March Violet, and the Early blue
violet. Usually used as a garnish for gourmet food, the
flower is the most commonly used part of the plant, although
many claim the whole plant is edible. Members of the violet
family can be found in yards, garden beds, cracks in
sidewalks, and more. BE SURE TO ONLY EAT WILD PLANTS as this
plant is often an ornamental in gardens and may contain a
variety of chemicals.

Seeds: Edible
Leaves: **Edible (not recommended)**
Flowers: **Edible**
Stalk: E**dible (not recommended)**

Practical Applications:
   1. Flowers are edible raw and may be used garnish.

Pineapple-weed

Abundance: ⭐⭐⭐⭐⭐
Seasons: **Spring Summer Fall**
Common Name: **pineapple-weed, wild chamomile**
Scientific Name: **Matricaria discoidea**
Family: **Asteraceae**
Nutrition:

Unknown nutritional information.

* = Very high amounts

Pineapple-weed, also known as wild chamomile, is one of the most common weeds that exist throughout urban areas of the state. Similar to chamomile, the plant can be used as a tea but also eaten raw when young.

Seeds: Edible
Leaves: **Edible (not recommended)**
Flowers: **Edible**
Stalk: E**dible (not recommended)**

Practical Applications:
1. Flowers are edible raw and may be used garnish or dried and used as a tea. They taste best raw when young, although bitter.
2. The plants can be eaten raw, but are quite bitter. They can be dried and crushed over meats to keep away flies and to reduce soilage.

Plantain

Abundance: ⭐⭐⭐⭐⭐
Seasons: **Spring, Summer**
Common Name: **Greater Plantain**
Scientific Name:
Plantago Major
Family: **Plantaginaceae**
Nutrition:

-Vitamin E*
-Vitamin K
-Calcium*
-Mangesium*
-Fiber*
-Vitamin A*
-Vitamin C*
-Manganese*
-Magnesium

* = Very high amounts

Plantains are quite abundant in the rural areas—they usually prefer well watered lawns or riverbanks. Tea made from its leaves can be used to treat diarrhea while replenishing the nutrients and minerals lost. It can be used as an anti-inflammatory, antioxidant, antibiotic, a boost to the immune system, and can be used to promote healing for wounds, sores and stings when leaves are applied. The sinews of mature plants can be used to make string as they are very pliable.

Roots: **N/A**
Leaves: **Edible**
Seeds: **Edible, but medicinal (see below)**
Stalks: **Edible, but not recommended**

Practical Applications:
1) Young leaves can be eaten raw. Older leaves are more tough and sour, so they can be boiled and eaten.
2) The seeds can be ground into a tea to treat sore throat and can promote bowel movements.
3) The leaves can be made into a tea, which can treat illness and replenish the body with important vitamins and minerals.

Purslane

Abundance: ⭐⭐⭐
Seasons: **Spring, Summer**
Common Name: **Pigweed**
Scientific Name:
Portulaca Oleracea
Family: **Portulacaceae**
Nutrition:

-Thiamin*
-Omega-3*
-Niacin*
-Vitamin B6*
-Folate*
-Vitamin A*
-Vitamin C*
-Riboflavin*
-Calcium
-Iron
-Magnesium
-Phosphorus
-Potassium
-Copper
-Manganese

* = Very high amounts

Purslane is a delicious and extremely nutritious plant found all throughout urban neighborhoods (in cracks in cement, weeds in garden beds, lawns, etc) and near bodies of water, such as streams and rivers. Purslane has more omega-3 fatty acids than any other leafy vegetable plant and is bursting with vitamins and minerals. It has a great taste and can be eaten as a salad or cooked in a variety of ways. Purslane has little yellow flowers and a soft foamy leaf.

Roots: **N/A**
Leaves: **Edible**
Flowers: **Edible**
Stalks: **Edible, but not recommended**

Practical Applications:
1) Purslane can be picked and eaten raw, boiled, steamed, fried and more. Can be added to soups and works great at a primary leafy green in salads.

Rose – Wild

Abundance: ⭐⭐
Seasons: **Spring, Fall**
Common Name: **Brier Hip**
Scientific Name: **Rosa Woodsii**
Family: **Rosaceae**
Nutrition:

-Vitamin E*
-Vitamin K
-Calcium*
-Mangesium*
-Fiber*
-Vitamin A*
-Vitamin C*
-Manganese*
-Magnesium
-Potassium

* = Very high amounts

Wild rose hips (the fruit of Roses) are one of Idaho's wild delicacies. These wild roses flower from June to July and the pink pedals are edible if the white base of the pedal is removed quickly. The rose hip turns red when they ripen in late August through September. Rose hips are extremely nutritious—they contain approximately 60 times the amount of Vitamin C compared to lemons and 25 times more than oranges, ounce to ounce. Wild rose can be found in forested areas, but prefer mountainous riverbanks.

Roots: **Edible (see below)**
Leaves: **Not Edible**
Seeds: **Not Edible**
Fruit: **Edible**
Stalks: **Edible, but not recommended**

Practical Applications:
1) Rose hips are red in color when ripe. Can eat raw or boiled with seeds removed.
2) The roots, if rinsed and minced, can be made into a tea. Native Americans used the tea for cold symptoms and fevers.

Salsify

Abundance: ★★★★
Seasons: **Spring, Summer, Fall**
Common Name: **Salsifies**
Scientific Name: **Tragopogon**
Family: **Asteraceae**

Nutrition:

-Calcium
-Mangesium*
-Dietary Fiber*
-Vitamin B6*
-Vitamin C*
-Manganese*
-Magnesium*
-Thiamin
-Folate
-Pantothenic Acid
-Phosphorus
-Potassium*

* = Very high amounts

Salsifies are quite an incredible survival plant both medicinally and as food. With yellow or purple dandelion-like flowers, salsifies can be found throughout Idaho's fields. (The purple salsifies are called "common salsify" and the yellow "yellow salsify". The common salsify often has larger and tastier roots.

Roots: **Edible (see below)**
Leaves: **Edible - Young**
Seeds: **Edible - Sprouting**
Stalks: **Edible - Young**

Practical Applications:
  1) The big roots can be eaten raw, boiled roasted or fried before flower stalks appear.
  2) Young leaves and flower buds can be eaten raw.
  3) Young stalks can be steamed or simmered, much like asparagus.
  4) Seeds can be collected, stored and used for sprouting.

Shepherd's Purse

Abundance: ★★★★
Seasons: Spring, Summer
Common Name: **shepherd's-purse**
Scientific Name: **Capsella bursa-pastoris**
Family: **Brassicaceae**

Nutrition:

Currently Unknown

* = Very high amounts

A member of the Brassicaceae family, Shepherd's-purse is an extremely common weed found throughout the whole state in all types of soils and climates. All parts of the plants are edible including the pods, seeds and roots. The plant has many applications as described below.

Roots: **Edible**
Leaves: **Edible**
Seeds/Pods: **Edible**
Stalks: **Edible**

Practical Applications:
1) The whole plant can be eaten raw at all stages of maturity, although it is best to cook when older (drier) due to consistency.
2) Pods and seeds can be eaten to give a peppery taste.
3) Roots can be eaten fresh, but may also be dried for future use
4) The ashes of plant, when burned, can be used as a salt substitute
5) Seeds can be parched for use as a flour when grounded.

Sow Thistle

Abundance: ⭐⭐⭐⭐
Seasons: Spring, Summer
Common Name: **sow thistle**
Scientific Name: **Sonchus**
Family: **Asteraceae**
Nutrition:

Currently Unknown

* = Very high amounts

There are a few varieties of sow thistle that can be found throughout the state, including Prickly sow thistle, Annual sow thistle and Perennial sow thistle. The plant is apart of the Sonchus genus, which includes dandelions and sunflowers. The plant is usually found around roadways and disturbed soils.

Roots: **N/A**
Leaves: **Edible**
Flowers: **Edible**
Stalks: **Edible**

Practical Applications:
1. The leaves and stalks of the plant are edible when young, but are best cooked as the plant matures. The flowers are edible raw.

Sunflower

Abundance: ⭐⭐⭐
Seasons: **Spring Summer Fall**
Common Name: **Sunflower**
Scientific Name:
Helianthus Annuus
Family: **Asteraceae**
Nutrition:

-Fiber
-Iron*
-Pantothenic Acid
-Vitamin B6*
-Niacin*
-Thiamin*
-Riboflavin*
-Omega Fatty Acids
-Phosphorus*
-Copper*
-Manganese*
-Magnesium*
-Potassium
-Protein*

* = Very high amounts

Sunflowers are common along roadsides and vacant fields throughout the state of Idaho. Most commonly found in sunny areas, sunflowers are very nutritious and all parts of the plant (aside from its tiny roots) are edible.

Roots: **N/A**
Leaves: **Edible**
Seeds: **Edible**
Stalk: **Edible**

Practical Applications:
1) Most obviously, sunflower seeds are edible, though most wild varieties have very small seeds. Can be eaten raw or roasted.
2) The stalks of sunflower plant can be boiled until soft and eaten plain.
3) The young flower buds in early to late spring can be eaten boiled until soft, similar to artichoke hearts.
4) Eating the leaves of a sunflower is not a wonderful experience, but if desperate, can be eaten boiled.

Thistle

Abundance: ⭐⭐⭐⭐
Seasons: **Spring**
Common Name: **Thistle**
Scientific Name: **Cirsium**
Family: **Asteraceae**
Nutrition:

-Fiber
-Ascorbic Acid*
-Chlorogenic Acid*
-Potassium*
-Inulin*
-Protein
-Calcium
-Cinarina*

* = Very high amounts

A commonly-found weed in disturbed soils of Idaho are Thistles. Though they are pests to many, they are also edible and may be a great source of food when in a survival situation. Thistles can be found virtually in any sunny climate and are mostly only edible during spring (or when plant is green). Be sure to use gloves while handling them!

Roots: **N/A**
Leaves: **Edible**
Seeds: **Edible**
Stalk: **Edible**
Flower Buds: **Edible**

Practical Applications:
  1) Use sharp knife to strip away outer skin from stalks. Inner stalks can be eaten raw, boiled or steamed.
  2) Flower buds (before matured) can be boiled. Peel flower bud after boiling. Soft inner core is edible.
  3) Leaves can be eaten boiled. Cut off thorns then boil.
  4) Seeds are edible. Can be eaten boiled, or if you have a machine to produce oil, 12 pounds of seeds will produce 3 pounds of oil.

WILD EDIBLE TREES

Aspen

Abundance: ⭐⭐⭐
Seasons: **Spring, Summer**
Common Name: **Aspen**
Scientific Name: **Populus Tremuloides**
Family: **Salicaceae**
Nutrition:

-Vitamin C*

* = Very high amounts

Aspens are fairly common in forested areas of Idaho, particularly northern parts of the state. They are both used as an ornamental tree throughout urban neighborhoods as well as throughout higher elevations. Similar to Cottonwood trees, many Native American tribes stripped the tender inner bark in springtime and used them as a sweet treat for kids. The tree also has incredible medicinal properties, such as killing parasitic worms and treating fevers, inflammation, pain, diarrhea, jaundice, urinary tract infections and more.

Leaves: **Edible — See Below**
Bark: **Edible - Inner**
Flower Buds: **Edible — See Below**

Practical Applications:
1) Use a sharp knife to strip away rough outer bark to gain access to soft, tender inner bark in springtime. Can be eaten raw.
2) Young leaf buds and catkins can be eaten raw and are very high in Vitamin C, though bitter.

Birch

Abundance: ⭐⭐⭐
Seasons: **Fall**
Common Name: **Black Birch**
Scientific Name: **Betula lenta**
Family: **Betulaceae**
Nutrition:

Currently Unknown

* = Very high amounts

Birch trees are very common in the moist temperate forests of the United States. There are many varieties of birch, though the most profitable of them all from a survival standpoint is the black birch. They can be found throughout forested areas and have a bark similar to that of cherry trees, while its other relatives, such as the mountain paper birch tree, are easily identifiable through its bright, white, paper-peeling bark.

Bark: **Edible — See Below**
Sap: **Edible**

Practical Applications:
1) The sap of birch trees are commonly made into syrup in colder climates where maple trees do not grow. Black Birch sap offers much higher quantities of sap in the spring time, which provides a wonderful source of clean water. The sap can be boiled and made into syrup.
2) Flour can be made by drying and grounding the inner bark.

Blue Spruce

Abundance: ⭐⭐⭐⭐
Seasons: **Spring**
Common Name: **Colorado Spruce**
Scientific Name: **Picea pungens**
Family: **Pinaceae**
Nutrition:

Currently Unknown

Blue Spruce is a commonly-found tree throughout the state in urban neighborhoods planted as an ornamental tree. The Blue Spruce offers a wide range of support to the survivalist. All evergreens, however, should be eaten in moderation.

Roots: **Not Edible**
Leaves: **Edible - See Below**
Stalk: **Edible - See Below**
Bark: **Not Edible - Medicinal**

Practical Applications:
  1) Young shoots can be eaten raw or cooked. Sources suggest not to eat the young needles with the shoots, but there has been no significant evidence showing any related health issues.
  2) Inner bark can be accessed through cutting away rough outer bark. Dried inner bark can be ground into a nutritious flour.

Chestnut

Abundance: ⭐⭐
Seasons: **Fall**
Common Name: **Chestnut**
Scientific Name: **Castanea dentata**
Family: **Fagaceae**
Nutrition:

-Vitamin C*
-Thiamin
-Vitamin B6
-Folate
-Riboflavin
-Potassium*
-Phosphorous
-Manganese*
-Copper*
-Omega 3 & 6 fatty acids

* = Very high amounts

A relative of the beech tree, Chestnuts are very common in urban areas of Idaho. There are many varieties of chestnuts that can be found throughout the state, but the most common and native tree is the American Chestnut. The tree produces edible nuts than can be harvested in the fall.

Leaves: **Not Edible**
Nuts: **Edible**

Practical Applications:
1) Only the nuts of the tree are edible. They can be harvested in fall, best after first frosts. They should be roasted before eaten. The nuts can be eaten whole or grounded into a flour.

Cottonwood

Abundance: ⭐⭐⭐⭐
Seasons: **Spring**
Common Name: **Balsam Poplar**
Scientific Name: **Populus Deltoides**
Family: **Salicaceae**
Nutrition:

Currently Unknown

Cottonwood trees are in the same family as poplars and aspens, and are one of the most despised trees throughout the warmer months of the year by many due to its allergenic properties, but the tree also has a sweet side. Many Native American tribes used the inner bark of the tree as a sweet treat for kids in the springtime while the sap was flowing. Cottonwoods can be found throughout the valleys both in urban neighborhoods or anywhere near water.

Roots: **N/A**
Leaves: **Edible**
Seeds: **Edible**
Stalk: **Edible**
Flower Buds: **Edible**

Practical Applications:
1) Use a sharp knife to cut off the rough outer bark to get access to the tender, sweet and translucent inner bark in spring time. Can be eaten raw in large quantities.
2) Young catkins can be eaten, though they may sometimes irritate skin.

Juniper

Abundance: ⭐⭐⭐
Seasons: **ALL**
Common Name: **Juniper**
Scientific Name: **Juniperus**
Family: **Cupressaceae**
Nutrition:

-Copper
-Chromium
-Calcium
-Iron
-Limonene
-Phosphorous
-Magnesium
-Potassium
-Vitamin C

* = Very high amounts

A very common tree in rocky, poor soil, Juniper provides incredible medicinal properties and offers a consistent source of food. There are many varieties of Juniper, though the most common variety found in Idaho is the "juniperus communus," or, common juniper. Although the berries are edible, it is not recommended to eat large amounts or for an extended period of time due to their strong medicinal properties. People with liver problems nor pregnant women should ingest any part of the Juniper.

Roots: **Not Edible**
Leaves: **Not Edible - Medicinal**
Fruit: **Edible — In Moderation**
Branches: **Not Edible**

Practical Applications:
1) Juniper berries are available all year round, though the sweetest berries have been through at least two seasons. Juniper berries have a very strong piney taste and are often better eaten dried or roasted.
2) Branches and leaves can be boiled into a tea, though it is extremely high in medicinal properties and can be toxic in high doses.

Maple

Abundance: ⭐⭐⭐
Seasons: **Spring**
Common Name: **Maple**
Scientific Name: **Acer**
Family: **Sapindaceae**

Nutrition:

-Potassium
-Calcium
-Magnesium
-Manganese
-Iron
-Zinc

* = Very high amounts

Maple is best known for it's syrup which is available in early spring time, when the tree wakes up and starts distributing its sap throughout its trunk. There are three commonly-found maples found throughout Idaho, including sugar and Norway maple. Planted both as an ornamental tree and found in the forest, maples can provide wonderful watery sap filled with probiotics and nutrients.

Leaves and Roots: **Not Edible**
Seeds: **Edible - Not Recommended**
Sap: **Edible**

Practical Applications:
1) Sap can be extracted from the tree in early-mid spring by carving a small but deep hole in the tree. You can carve a small wooden wedge to fit in the hole as a tap. Sap can be drank raw (similar to water infused with minerals) or it can be boiled down to a syrup.

Oak

Abundance: ⭐⭐⭐
Seasons: **Summer, Fall**
Common Name: **White Oak**
Scientific Name: **Quercus**
Family: **Fagaceae**
Nutrition:

-Fiber
-Protein*
-Vitamin B6*
-Manganese
-Copper
-Potassium
-Calcium
-Folate

* = Very high amounts

There are *many* varieties of oak that can be found throughout Idaho. The best tasting oak trees in Idaho are the white oaks, which include alba oak, bicolor oak, bur oak, muehlenbergii oak, and prinus oak. White oaks have the sweetest acorns of all other varieties, though they are still quite bitter. Oaks can be found all over the state, including urban and forested areas. The acorns were a major staple food for many Native Americans.

Roots: **Medicinal - Inner**
Leaves: **Not Edible**
Seeds: **Edible**
Bark: **Medicinal - Inner**

Practical Applications:
1) Acorns can be eaten raw, although they are quite bitter due to high levels of tannin. If eaten raw, remove outer shell before eating inner nut.
2) To remove bitterness, acorns can be roasted while in shell by placing them on stones placed over hot coals. An additional option for removing bitterness is by soaking the raw nuts (with shells removed) in multiple batches of water. This process can take 1-3 weeks.
3) Ground nuts can be used as a thickener for soups or baked into muffins, breads or pancakes.

Willow

Abundance: ⭐⭐⭐⭐
Seasons: **Spring, Summer**
Common Name: **Willow**
Scientific Name: **Salix**
Family: **Asteraceae**

Nutrition:

-Vitamin C*
-Salicin*

* = Very high amounts

While many varieties of willow are edible, they are mostly used medicinally. There are many varieties of willow, which mostly grow by lakes, rivers and streams, though many have been planted as an ornamental tree. Willows can appear as large weeping trees or shrub-like in appearance.

Roots: **N/A**
Leaves: **Edible – Young Shoots**
Bark: **Edible - Inner**
Stalk: **Edible – Young Shoots**
Flower Buds: **Edible – Young Buds**

Practical Applications:
1) The young shoots and leaves, inner bark and flower buds are edible. They can be eaten raw or cooked and are extremely high in Vitamin C.
2) Willow has many strong medicinal properties. As a warning, do not ingest tree in high dosages. People who are allergic or irritable to aspirin should not ingest willow.

WILD MEDICINE

Antibiotics & Antibacterials

Birch:
     Butulinic acid, found in the bark of the birch tree, has been shown to have antibacterial properties. The bark can be made into a tea and ingested in small quantities.

Curly Dock:
     The seeds and leaves of dock plants have anti-bacterial properties due to its high levels of anthraquinones. It can also act as a mild laxative and combat ringworm's and other fungi.

Juniper:
     Juniper berries contain antibiotic compounds and can be eaten raw or made into a tea to combat tumors.

Oak:
     Tannic acid, which can be found in acorns, is an anti-bacterial and anti-viral.

Plantain:
     Ingesting the raw leaves of plantains have anti-bacterial properties due to containing high levels of flavonoids.

Animal / Insect Bites

Burdock:
    Seeds of burdock can be used as a poultice to treat insect bites and snake bites.

Clover:
    Clover plants can be boiled in water to create a tea that can be used as an antidote for many poisonous bites and stings by scorpions and snakes.

Maple Tree:
    Tea made from the branches of maple trees can treat snake bites when applied both externally & internally.

Oak:
    Tea made out of oak bark can be used to treat insect bites.

Plantain:
    The juices of plantain leaves can be applied to the skin to treat snake bites, insect bites and stings.

Salsify:
    Tea made from all of the edible parts of the plant have been used to treat bites from coyotes both internally and externally.

Spruce:
    Spruce sap mixed with fat can be used to create a salve to treat insect bites.

Sunflower:
    Sunflower leaves can be applied topically as a poultice to treat spider bites and snake bites.

Blood Sugar

Burdock:

Burdock root has shown to reduce sugar levels in blood.

Dandelion:

The roots of a dandelion can be eaten raw or boiled and ingested to lower blood sugar, lower blood pressure, and lower cholesterol levels.

Juniper:

Juniper berries, when eaten raw, have been used to balance (lower) blood sugar levels that has been effected by adrenaline hyperglycemia.

Smooth Sumac:

Tea created from the berries of the smooth sumac was used to treat diabetes.

Blood / Organ Issues

Burdock:

    Ingestion of burdock root (boiled) has been shown to purify the blood, act as a liver tonic, treating liver, gout and kidney problems, high blood pressure, measles, vertigo, rheumatism and gonorrhea. Burdock root has also been used to dissolve bladder stones.

Clover:

    Red clover (*trifolium pratense*) can be eaten raw or made into a tea to act as a blood purifier, a blood thinner, or it can be used to remove toxins from the blood.

Dandelion:

    The roots of a dandelion can be eaten raw or boiled and ingested to lower blood sugar, lower blood pressure, and lower cholesterol levels. Tea made from the roots or leaves of dandelion can treat liver and urinary tract problems. Ingesting dandelion flowers can treat liver problems, such as jaundice.

Grape:

    Grape seeds and leaves can be cooked and ingested and used to prevent diseases of the heart and blood vessels, high blood pressure, varicose veins, heart attack, stroke, atherosclerosis, swelling and high blood pressure. It can also be used to treat complications due to diabetes as well as treat heavy menstrual and uterine bleeding.

Great Mullein:

    Tea made from mullein leaves can treat kidney infections. However, tea MUST be strained multiple times to protect throat against tiny fibers on leaves as they can cause irritation. WARNING: seeds of the great mullein are poisonous.

Cold Symptoms

Bergamot:
Native Americans have long used Burgamot as a treatment for colf and flu symptoms. Tea can be ingested made from the flowers and leaves of the plant. Very strong, so it's advised to use honey as a sweetener.

Catnip:
Making a tea out of the flowers and leaves of a catnip plant has been used to treat migraines and other headaches, as well as treating colds, upper respiratory infections, the flu, fever, hives, and more.

Clover:
Clover plants can be boiled in water to create a tea to be taken internally to treat cold symptoms such as fever, cough and sore throat.

Cottonwood:
The bark of cottonwood has been chewed to improve cold symptoms. Cottonwood bark can also be made into a tea for treating whooping cough and tuberculosis. Sticky resins from the flower buds can be collected in spring and ingested to treat coughs and pain.

Fiddlehead Ferns:
Being extremely high in Vitamin C, and flavonoid compounds like carotenes, fiddlehead ferns can provide protection from viral coughs and colds.

Juniper:
Native Americans have created tea using juniper branches and cones to treat coughs, pneumonia, fevers and colds. Juniper berries can also be chewed to treat colds. Native Americans would also burn juniper branches and inhale the smoke to relieve chest infections and colds.

Rabbitbrush:
Rabbitbrush roots can be boiled into a tea to treat cold symptoms, coughs and fevers. Tea can also be made from the leaves to treat colds and reduce fever.

Smooth Sumac:
Sumac berry tea had been used to treat fevers.

Spruce:

Sap from spruce trees can be boiled in water and used to treat coughing and sore throat. Needles can be boiled and chewed to relieve coughing. Tea made from the inner bark can be inhaled to relieve bronchitis.

Sunflower:
The flowers of sunflowers can be made into a tea to treat high fevers and headaches.

Thistle:
The leaves of the thistle plant can be made into a medicinal tea to treat cold symptoms such as fevers and strengthen the stomach.

Willow:
The bark of the willow tree can be made into a tea to treat fevers and headaches.

Cough / Throat

Black Raspberry:
　　Due to containing high levels of tannin, the roots and leaves of the black raspberry plant are extremely medicinal. They can be made into a tea to treat sore throats, gum inflammation and mouth ulcers. The leaves can be mashed and made into a wash to use as a mouthwash—both to gargle and wash mouth.

Bergamot:
　　Due to containing high levels of thymol, the active ingredient used in many mouthwashes, a strong tea made with bergamot flowers and leaves can treat mouth and throat infections caused by gingivitis and caries.

Chestnut:
　　Due to containing high levels of tannin, the leaves of the chestnut tree can be made into a strong tea to treat bronchitis (inflammation of the bronchi), coughing and asthma. Only small quantities should be taken at a time (3-4 tablespoons), but up to three glasses of tea is to be taken per day. Gargling the strong tea is a good method to use for inflammation and pain.

Cattail:
　　Chewing the leaves and stalks of cattail can treat or relieve sore throat and coughing.

Clover:
　　Clover plants can be boiled in water to create a tea to be taken internally to treat cold symptoms such as fever, cough and sore throat. The flowers of red clover can be made into a tea to treat asthma.

Cottonwood:
　　Sticky resins from the flower buds can be collected in spring and ingested to treat coughs and pain. Cottonwood bark can also be made into a tea for treating whooping cough and tuberculosis.

Juniper:
　　Native Americans would burn juniper branches and inhale the smoke to relieve chest infections. Native Americans also created a tea using juniper branches and cones to treat coughs and pneumonia.

Oak:

Oak bark tea can be used to relieve sore throats.

Plantain:

Plantain tea, made from seed stalks and leaves, have been used for hundreds of years as a treatment for coughs, laryngitis, bronchitis, tuberculosis, sore throat and mouth sores.

Rose:

Rose roots can be boiled into a tea that can be gargled to reduce swelling and treat sore throat and tonsillitis.

Spruce:

Sap from spruce trees can be boiled in water and used to treat coughing and sore throat. Needles can be boiled and chewed to relieve coughing. Tea made from the inner bark can be inhaled to relieve bronchitis.

Sunflower:

The flowers of a sunflower can be made into a tea to treat lung problems. The oil from sunflower seeds can be used to treat coughs and laryngitis.

Smooth Sumac:

The roots of smooth sumac can be chewed to relieve sore throats. The branches of the tree can be made into a tea to treat tuberculosis.

Cuts & Wounds

Bergamot:
Bergamot is a strong antiseptic, and therefor has been used by Native Americans as a treatment for skin infections and minor cuts/wounds. Make a poultice with leaves and apply to effected skin.

Chestnut:
Dried leaves can be crushed and mixed with water and be placed over cuts and wounds to prevent infection and promote healing.

Cottonwood:
Leaves can be applied to sores, boils, aching muscles and bruises that have been infected by maggots. Mixing flower buds (available in spring) with fat can be used as a salve that can treat skin infections and treat aching muscles.

Juniper:
Oils from juniper berries would often be used to protect wounds from flies by mixing them with fat to make salves.

Lambs Quarters:
The leaves of lambs quarters can be used as poultices to treat wounds, swelling and burns.

Salsify:
The white sap of salsify plants can be applied to open sores and wounds to stop bleeding and oozing.

Smooth Sumac:
The bark from the roots of smooth sumac can be used as a poultice to heal open wounds.

Spruce:
Sap from spruce trees can be mixed with fat to create a salve for treating cuts, rashes, scrapes and burns.

Willow:
Poultices made from the inner bark can be applied to insect bites, cuts, rashes, cancers, minor burns and scrapes.

Headache

Catnip:
    Making a tea out of the flowers and leaves of a catnip plant has been used to treat migraines and other headaches, as well as treating colds, upper respiratory infections, the flu, fever, hives, and more.

Great Mullein:
    Tea made from mullein stalks can treat migraine headaches. However, tea MUST be strained multiple times to protect throat against tiny fibers on leaves as they can cause irritation. WARNING: seeds of the great mullein are poisonous.

Lambs Quarters:
    The bruised leaves of lambs quarters can be applied to the head when experiencing headaches.

Plantain:
    Plantain roots can be boiled and eaten or made into a tea for treating headaches.

Rose:
    Rose petals can be eaten to treat headaches.

Sunflower:
    The flowers of a sunflower can be made into a tea to treat headaches.

Willow:
    Willow bark can be chewed or made into a tea to treat headaches.

Infections & Parasites

Aspen:
Tea made from aspen bark has been used to treat urinary tract infections and to kill parasitic worms.

Bergamot:
Bergamot is a strong antiseptic, and therefor has been used by Native Americans as a treatment for skin infections and minor cuts/wounds. Make a poultice with leaves and apply to effected skin. The phenolic compound thymol in bergamot has also been used to treat hookworms and other parasites.

Birch:
The bark of the birch tree can be made into a tar through heavy distillation and applied to skin to treat irritations and parasites.

Burdock:
Burdock leaves can be made into a wash (tea) that can treat skin infections.

Catnip:
Tea made out of the dried leaves and flowers of the plant can be ingested to treat worms.

Cottonwood:
Leaves can be applied to sores, boils, aching muscles and bruises that have been infected by maggots. Mixing flower buds (available in spring) with fat can be used as a salve that can treat skin infections and treat aching muscles.

Curly Dock:
Ingesting the leaves and seeds of dock plants can combat ringworm's and other fungi due to its high levels of anthraquinones.

Great Mullein:
Tea made from mullein leaves can treat kidney infections. However, tea MUST be strained multiple times to protect throat against tiny fibers on leaves as they can cause irritation. Flowers from mullein can be soaked in oil and applied topically to treat ear infections.

Plantain:
Plantain seeds and seed stalks can be used to make a

tea to treat intestinal worms due to containing high levels
of mucilage.

Spruce:

Sap from spruce trees can be mixed with fat to create a
salve for treating infections.

Thistle:

The leaves of the thistle plant can be made into a
medicinal tea to kill intestinal worms.

Smooth Sumac:

Tea made from smooth sumac berries has been used to
treat ringworm.

Pain & Inflammation

Aspen:
Due to its high levels of salicin, young leaves from the aspen tree can be ingested to relieve fevers, pain and inflammation.

Black Raspberry:
Due to containing high levels of tannin, the roots and leaves of the black raspberry plant are extremely medicinal. They can be made into a tea to treat sore throats, gum inflammation and mouth ulcers. The leaves can be mashed and made into a wash to use as a mouthwash—both to gargle and wash mouth.

Cattail:
Root-stocks can be made into a paste to treat inflammation. The root-stocks can also be made into a tea to treat abdominal pain.

Chestnut:
Due to containing high levels of tannin, the leaves of the chestnut tree can be made into a strong tea to treat bronchitis (inflammation of the bronchi), coughing and asthma. Only small quantities should be taken at a time (3-4 tablespoons), but up to three glasses of tea is to be taken per day. Gargling the strong tea is a good method to use for inflammation and pain.

Cottonwood:
Mixing flower buds from cottonwood (available in spring) with fat can be used as a salve that can treat skin infections and treat aching muscles. Sticky resins from the flower buds can also be ingested to treat coughs and pain.

Dandelion:
The roots of a dandelion can be eaten raw or boiled and ingested to reduce inflammation.

Great Mullein:
Tea made from mullein flowers can treat pain and act as a sedative. Tea made from mullein stalks can be used to treat cramping. Tea made from mullein leaves have been used as an anti-inflammatory due to its high levels of mucilage. However, tea MUST be strained multiple times to protect throat against tiny fibers on leaves as they can cause irritation.

Juniper:

Juniper berry tea has been used to reduce swelling and inflammation

Lambs Quarters:

The leaves of lambs quarters can be used as poultices to treat inflamed eyes.

Maple:

A tea made from maple tree branches can be applied externally and internally to reduce swelling.

Oak:

Oak bark can be chewed to relieve toothache pain.

Plantain:

Ingesting raw leaves and seed stalks of plantains can treat inflammation. The leaves can treat a variety of other issues including sprained and strained muscles, swollen joints and sore feet by heating leaves and applying them to the effected area.

Rose:

Rose leaves can be boiled into a tea to treat heartburn and headaches. The leaves can also be made into a salve to treat mouth sores. When mixed with wine, ground rose leaves can alleviate earaches, uterine cramping and toothaches. Rose seeds can be cooked and eaten to relieve sore muscles.

Salsify:

Ingesting salsify plants (refer to plant description for edibleness) has been used to relieve heartburn.

Sunflower:

The flowers of a sunflower can be made into a tea to treat swelling.

Willow:

The inner bark of the willow tree can be chewed or made into a tea to relieve pain. Willow has many similar chemical properties found in aspirin. Those who are allergic to aspirin should avoid taking willow.

Skin

Beech:
     The tar of beech trees (which can be made by distilling the bark) has been applied to the skin to treat excema and psoriasis. The leaves can be made into a poultice to treat scabs.

Birch:
     The bark can be made into a tea to treat eczema, warts and other skin conditions. The leaves can be made into a poultice and applied to scalp assist in preventing hair loss and dandruff.

Burdock:
     Burdock leaves have been applied to the skin as a poultice to heal burns, sores, and ulcers. Burdock leaves can also be made into a wash (tea) that can treat hair loss, skin infections, hives, psoriasis and eczema.

Cattail:
     Root-stocks can be made into a paste to treat wounds, burns, boils, sores scalds and inflammation.

Clover:
     Clover plants can be boiled in water to create a tea to be taken externally to treat skin diseases. Tea made from red clover flowers can be applied externally to treat skin issues such as sores, burns, ulcers, burns and athletes foot.

Cottonwood:
     Mixing flower buds from cottonwood (available in spring) with fat can be used as a salve that can treat skin infections. Leaves can be applied to sores, boils, aching muscles and bruises that have been infected by maggots.

Curly Dock:
     Dock leaves can be rubbed on the skin to aid rashes caused by stinging nettle. Ingesting the leaves and seeds of dock plants have also been suggested to treat warts and skin sores.

Dandelion:
     The milky sap from the dandelion root can be applied three times daily for 7-15 days in order to kill warts.

Great Mullein:

Mullein flowers can be soaked in oil and be used topically to treat warts. Mullein leaves and flowers can be used as a poultice to treat ulcers, hemorrhoids and tumors.

Juniper:

Juniper needles can be dried and made into a powder and applied to skin diseases.

Lambs Quarters:

The leaves of lambs quarters can be used as poultices to treat wounds, swelling and burns.

Oak:

Oak bark tea can be used to treat burns, rashes, cuts and scrapes.

Plantain:

The juices of plantain leaves can be applied to the skin to treat sunburns, sore nipples, poison-ivy rashes, cuts, burns and blisters. A strong tea made out of plantain leaves is said to treat dandruff.

Smooth Sumac:

The bark from the roots of smooth sumac can be used as a poultice to heal open wounds and ulcers. Leaves that are bruised and moistened can be applied to a variety of rashes, including ones caused by plant irritants such as poison oak, stinging nettles or poison-ivy.

Spruce:

Sap from spruce trees can be mixed with fat to create a salve for treating cuts, rashes, scrapes and burns.

Sunflower:

The flowers and leaves of a sunflower can be made into a poultice and/or a tea to treat blisters.

Thistle:

The leaves of the thistle plant can be made into a medicinal tea to apply externally & internally to treat ulcers, leprosy sores, pimples and rashes.

Willow:

Poultices made from the inner bark can be applied to insect bites, cuts, rashes, cancers, minor burns and scrapes.

Stomach Issues

Birch:
The bark of the birch tree can be made into a tea to treat diarrhea, dysentery and cholera.

Black Raspberry:
Due to containing high levels of tannin, the roots and leaves of the black raspberry plant are extremely medicinal. They can be made into a tea to treat severe diarrhea if taken multiple times throughout the day.

Catnip:
Making a tea out of the flowers and leaves of a catnip plant has been used to treat colic, indigestion, gas, gastrointestinal upset (GI), and as a tonic.

Cattail:
Flower buds ban be eaten to relieve diarrhea. Root-stocks from the cattail can be made into a tea to treat diarrhea and dysentery.

Chestnut:
Due to containing high levels of tannin, the bark of the chestnut tree can be made into a tea or crushed and eaten (with water) and used to treat diarrhea and dysentery if taken multiple times throughout the day.

Cranberry:
Eating the berry plain or made into a juice, cranberries have been used to treat urinary issues and help prevent bladder infections.

Dandelion:
The roots of a dandelion can be eaten raw, boiled or made into a tea to act as a laxative.

Oak:
Oak root bark can be boiled to create a tea to regulate bowel problems and to treat diarrhea.

Plantain:
Plantain seeds and seed stalks can be used to make a tea to treat diarrhea due to containing high levels of mucilage.

Rose:

Rose roots can be boiled into a tea and ingested to treat diarrhea and upset stomach.

Salsify:
Ingesting the white sap of salsify plants has been used to cure indigestion.

Smooth Sumac:
The bark of the smooth sumac tree can be made into a tea to treat diarrhea and dysentery.

Spruce:
Tea made from the inner bark of spruce trees can be used to treat stomach problems.

Thistle:
The roots of the thistle plant can be made into a medicinal tea and ingested to relieve dysentery and diarrhea.

Willow:
Willow bark may be chewed or made into a tea to treat digestive problems and diarrhea.

Urine / Bladder Issues

Aspen:
Tea made from aspen bark has been used to treat urinary tract infections.

Birch:
An infusion made from the leaves of the birch tree have been used as a cleansing agent to the urinary tract and is a diuretic. It has been used to dissolve kidney stones and to treat cystitis and other urinary tract infections.

Cattail:
Ingesting or chewing root-stocks can be used to increase urination.

Dandelion:
The roots of a dandelion can be made into a tea to stimulate urination and treat urinary tract issues.

Great Mullein:
Tea made from mullein roots can stimulate urination and be used as an overall medicine to improve the bladder. However, tea MUST be strained multiple times to protect throat against tiny fibers on leaves as they can cause irritation.

Juniper:
Juniper berries can be eaten raw to stimulate urination. Juniper berry tea can be used to cleanse kidneys.

Salsify:
Ingesting salsify plants (refer to plant description for edibleness) has been used to stimulate urination.

Smooth Sumac:
Tea made from the root bark can treat painful urination and assist with fluid retention in the body.

www.ingramcontent.com/pod-product-compliance
Lightning Source LLC
Chambersburg PA
CBHW060804270326
41927CB00002B/36